Himalayan Cats

A Pet Care Guide for Himalayan Cats

Himalayan Cat General Info, Purchasing, Care, Cost, Keeping, Health, Supplies, Food, Breeding and More Included!

By Lolly Brown

Foreword

As you ponder on choosing a pet for yourself or your family, it is utterly important that you look into finding out more about and understanding the sort of feline you will be bringing into the mix of your household. We want to help enlighten you and get to know more about the Himalayan cat better. This book is geared to give you informative, utilitarian tips on how to care of, socialize, groom, feed, and deal with your charming, blue-eyed feline.

One of the sweetest feline breeds around who will be ready to shower their human companions with equal respect, love and affection, the Himalayan cat is one of the most docile and undemanding of the feline sort that has been a continued favorite companion of many people all over the world. It is no surprise since the Himalayan cat is one of the charming cats around that would not demand too much fuss from their humans but does require the quiet reverence shared by close friends.

If you are looking for a long term companion to share your days with the Himalayan cat may be the feline you are looking for.

Table of Contents

Chapter One: Presenting the Himalayan Cat

There are some cats that prefer their company then there are those who choose to keep a few close friends within the family. The Himalayan cat is said to be one of the more quiet ones and a fairly independent sort. They are the kind of cats who prefer to keep the company of a few select people in the family and who reserve the love they give to the people who extend them the love and kindness they equally give.

Many people who chose to be just as independent opt to raise cats instead of canines as pets and if you are looking for a cat to gracefully join your ranks without great fuss you are correct to check out the Himalayan because quite unlike other pets the Himalayan cat is one sweet-tempered feline who loves the doting attention of its guardians and is happy to shower equal respect and attention to its human owners.

The Himalayan cat isn't the clingy sort of feline that would trip you up whilst you walk, but they are happiest when given a chance to catch up on some downtime with you as they sit on your lap or rest on your chest. It does not need a great amount of attention or endlessly mew unless they come into sudden pain or perhaps become agitated. They certainly enjoy the time they spend with you and it will not be unusual for you to find your Himalayan on chill mode when it is in an atmosphere where it can "let its hair down."

Aside from its docile and amiable personality, it's unique, and distinctive looks and appearance which only tops up its sweetness factor the loving nature of the Himalayan, as it is fondly called by feline aficionados, make the long-furred cat a consistently popular pick amongst cat lovers. Even canine lovers have understood the great companion it is and the Himalayan has changed the perception of many canine-folks about felines. It can easily work its way into the heart of an established feline-friendly dog you may have lived with for a while.

The Himalayan cat is a feline breed which is noticeably different in appearance with its mixture of Persian-Siamese features and traits. A combination of the two breeds; the Himalayan cat was developed sometime around in the 1930s and shares the sweet character traits of both natural occurring breeds. The time you decide to commit to a long term companionship with and take on the responsibility of being a caregiver to a pet, you will need to keep in mind that you will have to make a few major adjustments to your time and schedule to make room for the animal you will be taking in.

The time that you are willing to invest, the patience it will take for smooth integration to the family and the effort required from you will be important to the foundation of your Himalayan's life. Financially, taking in an animal is usually compared to raising a baby or a child. Suffice to say, that raising either, does not come cheap - you will have to be ready for this fact. Consider and expect to add the amount it will cost to fund their upkeep and health care of a new pet because this will certainly take a considerable chunk of money from your monthly financial budget.

Make sure that you are able to set aside and make time for the things that the cat will need from you. No matter what breed, all felines require being taken care of with utter and thoughtful care beginning with the provision of its nutritional care, everyday maintenance routines (feeding, grooming, scooping out its poop-box, etc.), as well as periodic and regular visits to the vet, your Himalayan cat will require your attention to do these tasks.

Consider yourself lucky if you are given a break in adopting one of these adorably docile, luxuriously soft, furry felines because Himalayan cats are quite expensive and are not easy to come by. They are sought for their unique appearance and show quality breed by many cat aficionados. Aside from these traits they are also popular with pet lovers because of their loving nature.

You are probably in strong consideration of procuring a Himalayan Cat and wish to learn more about them. Find out about the Himalayan cat and learn what it takes to get one added to the dynamics of your household. This is written to enlighten and help you as you research and determine whether you are ready to take on the responsibilities of being caregiver to the sweet, soft-voiced feline. And we hope that this book helps you get closer to making a decision. An addition to the family mix always entails a good measure of adjustment, schedule-wise as well as a shift the area of household cash flow. Taking on a pet will require a lot of commitment from a potential owner.

Whichever breed you choose to take in and raise, keep in mind that raising a pet requires time, patience and love. Himalayan cats require your attention every day to help in maintaining its cleanliness and good health. Much like other pets, the Himalayan cat needs care which will have to become a part of your daily, weekly and monthly routine. Himalayan cats are fairly sociable cats that prefer gentle play therefore they will not be very kindly toward rough play and round housing. They do however integrate well into families with children who have been taught to treat animals with kindness and respect.

Should you be a household raising existing pets, whether they are and older feline-friendly dog and/or another breed of cat, it would please you to know that the long-haired, blue-eyed feline can get on well with other cat-friendly pets, with gentle introduction. It is to be said though that Himalayan cats much prefer the tranquil quiet of its day, enjoying lap time with the one they trust and with whom they enjoy company.

It is highly recommended that you raise a Himalayan cat indoors. Raising them inside the confines of your comfortable home will avoid unwarranted, violent attacks by animals bigger than they are. This also avoids them from contracting disease with possibly sick feral cats and strays. Another reason to keep them indoors is that they are adorably lovely and could get catnapped. The last thing you want is heartache in the form of losing it.

The Himalayan cat is a sweet cat that languishes and adores attention and would typically want to take part and interact with its humans as well as children who show it love. You will soon find out that it is pretty independent and can be left alone for an extended period of the day. The Himalayan cat is most content when around its humans and loves nothing more than to lap sit with you or lounge about in the general area of your presence. It is an inquisitive little thing who loves to help you with your day, piping in quietly about the things you are doing. It is sweet-tempered cat who is hard to ignore the minute it curls up next to you and asks for your attention.

Chapter Two: Get to Know the Himalayan Cat

The Himalayan cat is a breed of feline that was developed through human intervention in the United States. It is a breed developed in 1931 by cross-breeding the Siamese and the Persian with the intention of marrying the blue eyes of the Siamese and the colour - points of the Persian cat. Initially done to determine the method of how the colour-point genes were passed on and selective breeding developed the longhaired cats, complete with the unmistakable colour points.

Through the initiative of Harvard Medical Researcher Clyde Keeler and cat breeder Virginia Cobb the Himalayan cat resulted. Both these individuals responsible for the breed bred the cats back to Persians intending to build a foundation breed. And once the Himmies bred true, they sought recognition for the cats.

The Himalayan cat breed by the some of the most renowned cat-fanciers association in the United States and the world, like The International Cat Association (TCA), American Cat Fanciers Association (ACFA), the Cat Aficionado Association (CAA) and Cat Fanciers' Association (CFA) today. Some recognize them as a category on their own, whilst the rest of the associations classify them separately.

The Himmies were given recognition by the CFA as a breed on its own in 1957. However, this sole classification was revoked in 1984, reclassifying them as a Persian with colour variety. This goes the same for the ACA as well as the ICA. All three of these cat associations currently recognize the Himalayan cat as a member of the Persian group, inclusive of the Exotic Shorthair and the Persian cat. These days, the Himmie is allowed to be outcrossed with Persians or Exotic Shorthairs. However crossing a Himmie with a Siamese is now out of the picture and is no longer a part of the breeding program for Himalayan cats.

It would good you good to know is that they are able to easily integrate themselves into families and households that extend it loving respect. With proper integration coupled with a lot of loving patience, they are able to share space with other pets that are able to get along with them. The Himalayan cat is certainly a loving sort who would be happy to share love and attention with its other furry pals but the beautiful creature thrives most especially during its downtime with its human family.

The Himalayan Cat Breed - A History in Brief

Little is known of the origins of the exotic Himalayan cat until the 1930's when the breeders searched for ways to combine the distinct looks and personalities of the Persian and Siamese cats.

It is believed that the Persian long-haired cats come from the Pallas's cat, a wild cat which calls central Asia its natural home and that is naturally without stripes or spots and possess luxuriously long supple fur. There is, little to no ontological or other evidence for this supposition. The Himalayan is said to be possibly more a result of the long-haired domestic cat which were purposefully chosen by man in the hopes of successfully combining and developing the distinct looks and characteristics of each feline.

Ongoing examinations are being conducted in order to reveal the descendants of the Himalayans. One research and experimentation example is the rare colour variety of the American mink which was said to have been found living in a ranch in Nova Scotia and commonly called the marbled variety sort due to the distinct distribution of pigment pattern similar to that found in some other species who sport similar patterns; examples to cite are the Siamese cat and the Himalayan mouse.

The Himalayan came about through human intervention and is a breed which was developed by cat fancier Virginia Cobb and scientist Dr. Clyde Keeler. The first ever Himmie came about during the fourth-generation cross-breeding try of the Massachusetts-based Newton Cattery member and the Harvard Medical School tandem of Ms. Cobb and Dr. Keeler.

The Himalayan Cat - Born in the USA

Work to formally establish a breed with combined Persian and Siamese traits, explicitly for the cat fancy, began in the United States in the 1930s at Harvard University, under the term Siamese–Persian, and the results were published in the Journal of Heredity in 1936, but were not adopted as a recognized breed by any major fancier groups at the time. Brian Sterling-Webb independently developed the cross-breed over a period of ten years in the UK, and in 1955 it was recognized there as the Longhaired Colourpoint by the Governing Council of the Cat Fancy (GCCF).

The job to establish the breed formally, combining Siamese and Persian cat traits, solely for the intention of defining the colour pattern points as well as each of the breed's character traits, started in the USA in the 1930's. It was in Harvard University where tests and development was conducted and where the cat was classified under Siamese-Persian category. Results of the development of the Himmie were later published in 1936 in the Journal of Heredity. At this time, no cat association had yet recognized the breed.

It was much later on when an independent breeder in the United Kingdom, named Brian Sterling-Webb, developed the cross-bred cat over a period of 10 years, and eventually got its recognition by the Governing Council of the Cat Fancy (GCCF) as the Longhaired Colourpoint.

Continued breeding efforts were carried out separately in the United States in the 1950's by a breeder simply known and remembered as Mrs. Goforth. It was through the efforts of the good Mrs. Goforth that the

Himalayan Cat received recognition of the breed from the Cat Fanciers Association toward the tail end of 1957.

The interest in giving the long-haired Himalayan the colouration of the Siamese was of the main interest of many breeders back then and this reinforced the stock breed through outbreeding it to Persians, with intent to keep the dominant traits of the Persian cat. In the 1960's, some breeders began re-introducing Siamese cats to the breed in the attempt to produce less of the Persian-looking cats. The concerted aim to re-establish the Himalayan cat breed along the more Persian-like appearance and trait came about in the 1980's. This effort caused the breed to be merged as a variant of the Persian breed in some of the more notable cat registries in the early-mid 80's.

Once this was established breeders were better equipped with knowledge and facilities to create a conducive atmosphere for the cats and from then a lot were learnt about the personality, habits, the medical issues, and traits of the Himalayan cat. Whilst on the lookout for a Himalayan cat, do remember that it is called other names like; the Himalayan Persian or the Colourpoint Persian.

The Himalayan Cat - Feline Lineage, Apperance and Distinctions

Very little is known of the Himalayan cat, except for the information gathered beginning in the 1930's when it was initially developed in the United States and later in the 1950's in the United Kingdom. There is almost no record in early literature and photographical representation to give indication of how the cats came about.

As with other Persian breed, there are currently two sorts of Himalayan cats; the doll-faced Himalayan and the peke-faced Himalayan (also known as the ultra-typed Himalayan). The peke-faced Himalayan has more of the squashed-looking, tightly-cropped facial features as opposed to the traditional Himalayan.

Show Himalayans have a break on their nose much like the peke-faced Persian. They share the same large, round eyes with its nose leather set between its eyes. Typical of the breeder Himalayans are their longer noses, as opposed to the show Himalayans, and they have a longer muzzle. Breeder Himalayans also have notably smaller eyes as compared to show Himalayans. All of them are nonetheless, Himalayans by natural selection.

Things to Know About the Himalayan Cat

Himalayan cats are called various names depending on the registries it is under. Some registries would call them Himalayan Persian whilst others would classify the Himmies as Colourpoint Persians. This sort of cat breed is certainly one of the more adorable looking felines you will ever set eyes on. Not exactly one what one would describe as high maintenance since the Himmie is docile, mild mannered, amicable, intelligent, quiet and playful.

A calming ritual you can nurture with your own Himmie is grooming time. And you can be sure that you and your Himalayan cat will enjoy a lot of these quiet times together. Grooming and brushing your Himalayan is a way to enjoy some downtime with them. Grooming can be a fun time for both you and your cat allowing both of you to catch up with each other.

Nail trimming can be kept at a bare minimum and on a need-to basis because it is recommended to that you raise your Himmie indoors. Providing it with a scratch post should suffice. Should you feel the need for your himmie to be given nail trims, a routine done fortnightly should suffice, along with the aid of a scratch post. Ear cleaning is a needful requirement which should be carried out religiously to avoid parasites from taking over your beloved feline.

You will need to learn to give your Himalayan cat baths to avoid it from getting shoddy and to allow its long hair to stay soft and supple. Given your support and patient, gentle introduction Himmies could easily integrate with other cats and mature, cat-friendly dogs.

Chapter Three: Things to Consider Before Buying a Himalayan Cat

A crucial factor when choosing to take in a pet for yourself or your family is the compatibility of pet and guardian. The individual and family dynamics of pet and humans need to be considered to ensure a painless and fuss-free transition of integration. Your research now is vital at this point as you make a decision.

Keep in mind that just like other pets, the Himalayan cat requires its own special care and attention. As we are all prone to medical conditions so is the Himalayan cat prone to theirs. It is imperative that you know, remember and remind those sharing a home with a Himmy that the cat has a tendency to develop PKD due to its Persian ancestry. It is therefore important to get both Himalayan parents tested before they mate to avoid passing on the defective gene to their offspring. Getting in touch with upstanding breeders will shave off the possibility of this, and you will know more about how to find the best possible breeders in order to avert PKD in your Himmy.

This next section aims to reveal more of your compatibility to the Himalayan cat and will inform you better on what it would need from you in order to thrive in the new environment you shall be introducing to it.

Do Himalayan Cats Get Along Well with Other Pets?

Almost all felines - as with most pets on four legs - are innately territorial animals. They have the tendency to take stock of their environment and they like to stake claim of spaces and areas whilst in the process of getting familiar with a new home. If you are the kind of owner who has more than one established pet and is thinking of adding one more, knowing the traits of the Himalayan cat will be important because himmies do not take well to chaotic environments and enjoy a tranquil lifestyle.

A lot of animal lovers keep an open mind about adding new pets into their homes. Pet owners with established pets get worried about peaceful integration of new animals into homes with existing pets. Unfortunately many owners all too frequently make the mistake of not doing the right research they need to do prior to bringing home a new pet into their family.

This can result to utter frustration and exhaustive effort on the part of the owner and anxiety and stress to the animals. To prevent this scenario prepare yourself and understand the pros and cons of integrating your pets. Learn to ask the right questions to the proper people and the hurdle of introducing a new Himmy cat to your established pets may not be too much of a task.

You may notice quite a bit of tension and excitement in the air upon the initial meeting and integration of your pets. It is not unusual to experience a bit of a commotion at the onset of the meeting. You will also notice a lot of curious sniffing at the very least and a bit of resistance as well. It is at this point of introduction when your patience and supervision will be absolutely crucial.

Himalayan cats are sweet-tempered, docile, relaxed and highly intelligent felines who dote on the attention of their humans. Himmies are not the sort who would easily get along with other pets since they do enjoy their space and the calm they create in it. They are able to accustom themselves to new accommodations, and guardians, with time. Your attentive assistance is crucial at this time. With patience and mindful integration you'll find them to easily blend in well with other cat-friendly pets you may already have at home.

If you are a family with existing pets it would serve you well to know that Himalayan cats will possibly need more time than most to learn to get along with other cat-friendly pets. It may be possible to mix in the company of a laid-back Basset Hound, a relaxed Havanese, or a playful Pomeranian, all of which love the company of other pets. The gentle Newfoundland giant is also a good cat-friendly dog choice who may be more than willing to share space and attention with a new Himalayan cat addition to the home.

Should You Opt for More Than One Himalayan Cat?

Himalayan cats are docile, friendly felines who can be open to enjoying the company of other Himmies. These special cats are given a better chance of getting along with each other better if they grow up together. So if you are bent on getting more than one, a pair is more manageable together in the long run. Coupled himmies who have lived together have been noted to be fairly independent of each other but will enjoy the company of another Himmy when playtime is the order of the day.

You will get to know more about how to integrate a Himmy into your household in the next few chapters. However, keep in mind that if you have an established Himmy lording over your home, you will still be required to be the mediator during induction. All cats share a similar trait of being territorial animals and may display indications of anxiety or distress once they sniff out a stranger, whether they are human or the four-legged sort.

Make the introduction period smooth by cushioning the situation with your presence. Gently integrate the new Himmy with the established Himalayan following the detailed tips you will find in this chapter. This being said, a Himalayan cat enjoys being in the company of their human caregivers and will be ready to shower its owners with the love and affection it has to give. If you are the busy cat-lover who has a lot on their plate and can't always be present for your long-haired furry friend most times of the day, then it would truly be ideal to give your Himalayan cat the company of another Himmy.

When Introducing a Himalayan Cat in a Household with another Cat

You may have probably noticed that most felines are quite territorial - that is if your household already has an existing feline pet. They like to stake their claim on spaces around the home and will seem agitated when another pet or strange human is in the home. You will have to allow your old feline buddy time sufficient enough in order for it to get used to the new Himmy addition.

Here are some utilitarian tips you can use to help the transition of integration along:

- Give the cats ample time to get used to each other's scent. This means, literally give them time to sniff each other out. First of all you want to place the new cat inside a separate room and allow the established feline to get used to the scent of their new companion from the safety of the other side of the closed door.

- Give the established cat a swatch of cloth or blanket the new cat was in recent contact with to sniff out. Place the swatch of cloth or blanket near or around the established cat and allow it time to investigate the new scent to help it get used to the smell.

- The next phase of introduction entails placing both cats in the same room with a safe space between them in separate corners. Your watchful eye and supervision as well as the help of another family member will be crucial at this point. Quietly observe how they act and react when they see each other. Should you be alone and are carrying out the integration by yourself, make use of a cat carrier and allow the existing pet to get closer to the new one.

- Make use of an indoor fence. Put both cats in the space with the indoor fence acting as barricade. Take note of the body language of both cats. Observe how each of the cats act and react around each other. You will know that the barricade can be eliminated altogether when they are relaxed and calm.

- As soon as the walls come down and they are in the same space with no boundaries between them and if they seem calm around each other, you can begin encouraging the next phase of integration, which is play. Use a feather-teaser and begin play by slowly moving the feather teaser from side to side, up and down. This will get both of their attention and you soon will see that a little gentle play will pave the way for them to overcome their anxiety toward each other.

One of Each for Both

In order to welcome the new addition to your home warmly and to assure the existing pet of its value and reassure it that it is just as loved and wanted, make sure that you provide them each with separate sundries they will be using often.

- Give separate and identical feeding bowls and water dishes for each of your pets. Position them strategically in separate spaces in the same room where they both can eat their meals together with a good distance between.

There is nothing more a feline dislikes more than feeling less important than the other pet:

- Allot each with separate, identical beds in the same room. Giving them identical beds will teach them to share and mix it up when they are in a good sharing mood.

- Just like us, your four-legged cat friends need to have separate toothbrushes. There is a reason why toothbrushes are personal, and that is the prevention of spreading mouth infections which could be transmitted by sharing toothbrushes. You will be wise to invest on a good pet toothbrush for each of your cat's oral hygiene.

Cats are by nature very uncomfortable about doing natures business in a soiled litter box. They are even iffier about doing their business where another cat just went. This could lead to agitation and constipation. Provide your cats with unsoiled, unused litter boxes and position them around the home where they are strategically visible to the cats. Be mindful of the cats body language and place them to the areas when you notice that they are about to do their business or when they pose to urinate.

Litter boxes a-plenty. The ideal ratio of litter box to cat should be 2:1. This may seem a tad much to you, but, this is an important fact you need to be aware of before you make your decision to add another cat to the mix. Remember to regularly clean the litter boxes as cats hate going in a dirty box.

A soft hypoallergenic blanket they can both share will serve as a good romp-area for a game of Hide and go Seek. Not only would it a be a comfortable space to lounge and sleep in, it can be a good source of exercise for your cats as they do have a love for hiding, sneaking up on and playfully jumping at their fellow-felines and human buddies.

There are many other things your cats can share apart from a place in your heart. Beds which they may choose to interchange, or share a cuddle in as well as toys. Cats will typically be curious about what the other cat owns and could exchange feeding and drinking bowls as well. This is the reason why providing each with their own is important. Cats are perceptive animals and making one feel less important than the other should be avoided. There is no room for favoritism.

- Make separate perches for each of them. Position these cat perches strategically in rooms to dissuade your cats from perching on high bookshelves and display cabinets. Himalayan cats are intelligent and you can easily train them to use their perch instead of sitting atop the refrigerator.

- Create perches at home by recycling old wood and fixing them onto walls with sturdy wall brackets. Make sure that the perches are fastened and attached to the walls securely. Take pains in making sure that the perch is sturdy so that jumping on and off the perch is safe for the cats. Test that the perch you make doesn't dislodge easily to avoid any falling accidents.

- Conflict is an ever present possibility in all families and one which you will have to stand as mediator. When mediating quarrels it is best to draw attention away from the fight by loudly clapping your hands and calling out the names of your warring feline buddies. You can also use a water bottle sprayer to separate the two hotheaded felines to allow both some time to cool off.

- Cats in conflict will depend on their caregivers to resolve the conflict. One smart way to ease any tension is to groom both cats at the same time. Give both of your felines the same amount of attention and

care. Speak to both of them while you groom them.
When cats are in conflict, take the opportunity to give
them both a calm brush-massage whilst speaking to
them in calm, loving tone.

The Cost of Taking in a Himalayan Cat

Taking in a new member to join the household ranks
will surely entail a shift in your monthly budget. Although
Himalayan require very little maintenance apart from daily
coat brushing, teeth cleaning, the occasional cleaning of the
ears, face wiping and periodic nail trimming, it will need to
be inoculated and be brought for periodic visits to the vet.

Procuring a Himalayan kitten could set you back
anywhere from $400-$600 and this price hikes up
considerably more if the Himalayan is bred by a reputable
breeder. A good breed from a high-end cattery could fetch
for a higher price, and this goes the same for show cats
which could cost up to about $1,500. Factor in vaccination
and medical fees, transportation costs, should you be getting
a cat from a remote location or out of state.

This next section is aimed to aid you in determining if
you are financially ready and capable of taking in a
Himalayan cat. You will find an overview and a rundown of

what you could potentially be spending on a Himalayan cat if your heart is set to add one to your blend. We have included the costs of vet care, medicine, treats and toys, food, grooming, feeding and sleeping equipment as well as sundries it would need for its daily maintenance, hygiene and grooming.

Initial Costs

On average a Himalayan cat coming from a reputable cattery or breeder would set you back anywhere from $500-$1500. Keep in mind that you want to find an honest breeder as this will save you money in the long run. Unscrupulous breeders can potentially pass on genetically ill cats bred of parents who both carry the dominant gene. This will result in future medical bills and avoidable health issues for the cat.

You will read more about the importance of knowing the history of your Himalayan cat as you read further. Adding a pet to the family is almost equal to caring for a child - minus the school tuition and back talk. Consider your finances and how much you can afford on a monthly to yearly basis. Some of the expenses you want to consider would be the initial inoculation cost, fees to cover neutering or spaying, toys and grooming supplies when you set your budget aside.

The Pros and Cons of Cat Ownership

It has been known and said that cats bring with them certain healing properties like staving off depression and sadness. They bring about a form of joy that is priceless and unmatched. Owners of cats would attest to this and this is even backed up by scientific facts.

Getting to know the breed and sort of pet you want to take in will allow you to make a sound decision about your acquisition. To determine if you are ready to take on the responsibility for the care of one we have come up with information about the positive and negative sides of acquiring or adopting a Himalayan cat.

As a new or existing pet owner, you must ask questions when needed and study up on the specifics of the pet you want to take in in order to empower yourself to find out about everything you need to know in relation to taking care of your new pet. Knowing the cat's parental history, the breeding methods employed by breeders to develop the pet and the possible medical conditions an animal may be prone to are some of the more pressing questions that will need answers.

Pet ownership entails responsibilities for the long haul so it is just right that you ask the breeder and a pet health care provider about possible illnesses your new pet might develop. You have to take it upon yourself to find out what to do, and to avoid in order keeping your cat safe and healthy.

All animals can suffer from anxiety and stress especially if taken away from their mother too soon when they are too young. As a pet owner you need to position yourself and prepared to recognize these symptoms of anxiety in your pet.

Stress and anxiety are signs of fear and insecurity. These feelings are manifested through actions like skittishness. They have poor eating habits which results to them having a weak immune system. They may hide and shy away from company and not develop socially. Make sure that your Himmie is at least 12 weeks old and that it has weaned off its mother before you take it home. This gives them a greater chance of gaining a good footing and it allows for a more balanced feline.

With the guarantee of a breeder, your 12 week old Himalayan should have been vaccinated and this would ensure that the cat has been socialized well enough before parting it with its mother. The cat would have been seen by a vet and, ideally, would have already been given a clean bill of health.

Himalayan cats are fairly independent felines and are able to entertain themselves during your periods of absence. Provide it with enough toys and cat-equipment so as to keep them busy and engaged during your temporary absence and you will come home to a cat that will dote on your presence. They have a tendency to either be active for a few hours and will want to lounge around when they are all tuckered out. Make sure that you allot a decent amount of your time and spend it with your cat. Cats get anxious and develop an inferiority complex when not given attention by their owners. It also defeats the initial socialization it has learnt. They are touchy little creatures who are attuned to the feelings of their owners.

Make it a point to have a medical cat-specialist on your speed dial in case of emergencies. Not only will a vet be able to give you the low down on the needs of your new pet Himmie, your vet is also a good source of feline-related information like the type of diet they would need, the medical conditions they may develop and give medical attention to the animal when needed. They are the best people to give you tips on how to groom, feed and raise your cat. The Himalayan cat is an intelligent cat with a playful disposition. It is a graceful player who will give you endless hours of joy simply watching it go at play. Your Himmy cat is a great anti-depressant.

The Himalayan cat is prone to respiratory infections due to its shortened face, especially those who are meant to be show cats. Brachycephalic cats are more prone to breathing difficulties and many people consider this facial condition to be a disability. Feline advocacy groups are raising more concern about the breeding of short faced cats and have raised their voices calling for a radical shift in breeding methods. If you are bent on getting a Himalayan cat, be advised that you should expect a probable problem with their health.

Another cause for medical concern in brachycephalic cats is that they have tear ducts that are distorted. This means that moisture from their eyes drain down their nose instead of their eyes. This can cause dermatitis if the cat is not groomed daily and at the least cause unsightly fur staining. Because of their shortened skull, their eye sockets tend to bulge, making them susceptible to congenital problems as well as eye damage.

This can be very painful for Himmies. The possibility of eye irritation in Himmies is exponentially greater because of their bug-eyed appearance. Due to its Persian anscestry, Himalayan cats are also prone to polycystic kidney disease - this is an inherited medical condition passed on by either or both parents of the Himalayan. PKD is a condition which causes enlarged kidneys as well as kidney dysfunction. Make sure that your Himmie kitten is given a DNA test and that it has tested negative for PKD. Another grave concern for your Himalayan cat is its eyes. Progressive retinal atrophy (PRA) is a passed on mutation typically seen in Persians which generally leads up to total blindness around 16 weeks of age. The breeder you deal with should be well aware of this gene mutation and Himalayan cats suffering from PRA should either be spayed or neutered.

Himalayan cats lead a moderate lifespan of about 15 years in spite of its compromised respiratory sytem. The Himmy has a hard time dealing with heat and is therefore advised to be kept indoors most of the year especially if you live in a country with tropical climate. Aside from being kept indoors in order for it to keep a good regulated bdy temperature, the Himalayan cat is best raised in the safety of your home to avoid attacks from large animals and to avoid it from getting whisked off by strangers as well as exposure to elemental and environmental dangers.

Chapter Four: Purchasing and Selecting a Himalayan Cat

Himalayan cats are adorable little creatures of habit and a picture of content when they are in their element. You will notice their distinct playful mannerisms and they would elicit laughter and joy with their cat antics and shenanigans. Himmies are known to follow you around the house and inspect the things you do with great curiosity. They would hardly ever pipe in but when they do, you will be sure that you won't be able to ignore their soft voices.

It will be hard to ignore your Himalayan cat because they are attentive little things you do and will keep you company as you go about your day at home. Himalayan cats will not think twice about showing you love as long as you take care of giving them time and attention. It will not be unusual for them to get into playful mischief at times.

They are the sort of playful and inquisitive cats who love your attention. They are highly trainable cats and are intelligent beyond compare. Himmies have been a Hollywood favourite and has shred the limelight with many notable actors of the silver screen. They have also been the star of their own web-based videos with their own set of followers. An endless supply of hours upon hours of Himalayan cat videos is testament to their ever-growing popularity.

Cats on video are as close as you can get to seeing pure joy with the naked eye. The Himalayan breed, clever to the bone, sweet and soft spoken, has truly carved a niche in the World Wide Web as an adorable feline. Having read this far, it is now time for us to help you find an upstanding breeder. Learning the breeder trade will empower you to know who to deal with so that you are handed a healthy Himalayan cat when the time is right. Getting your cat from a good breeder will be a milestone you will remember as a good day. Once you fall in love with your Himmy, you can be sure that you will never be the same again.

The innocence of the Himalayan cat may allow you to remember to appreciate the simpler things in life. Its mild demeanor and its relaxed, easy going manner may just influence and encourage you to put on the brakes and smell the roses. The manner in which it leads a lifestyle of contentment may just inspire you to reassess your own level happiness. The friendly disposition it possesses may just remind you to smile a bit more and spread kindness. The Himalayan cat will not only change the way you live your life, its very presence may just be what you need to soothe your frayed nerves and calm your everyday worries.

Find out where you can go to and the sort of breeder you want to talk to in order to get a Himalayan in the pink of health. You will also find in this chapter useful tips on how to cat-proof your home.

Where to Acquire a Himalayan Cat?

Himalayan cats are susceptible to many medical conditions, one of which stem from their Persian ancestry. The health issues of the Himalayan cat could cause not only heartache but also a mountain of medical bills if you are not aware of its background. Dealing with breeders who employ humane methods of breeding is crucial at this stage.

First off, it is not advisable to get a Himalayan from a pet store as they will not be able to properly give you important information about the history of the cat. These are details about your cat that will prove to be important to its well-being and health in the future. It is imperative that you find an upstanding breeder who would have employed only the best standards.

If you have deep pockets and a great big heart, you can look into getting your Himalayan addition at a pet shelter. Pet shelters may or may not have historical information about the cat of your interest, but taking in an adult cat and rescuing it from an uncertain future would be a reward on its own.

What to Remember When Choosing a Reputable Breeder

Finding a trustworthy Himalayan cat breeder will minimize any worries you may have about the health and well-being of the cat. Dealing with one will give you some reassurance that you will not be taking home an ill kitten.

The following are tips on how to tell an upstanding breeder from shady ones:

- You will want to network with other Himalayan cat owners to start off. Previous and current owners of Himalayan cats can be some of the best sources of breeder information. In addition you can stay in contact with groomers, and veterinary clinics for additional options.

- Collect information about breeders in your local and look up breeders with websites. You can study their worthiness by scrutinizing their feedback, ranking, reputation and license.

- Don't be taken for a ride - ask questions. And ask lots of relevant ones.

- Ask about the breeder's breeding program. Inquire of their breeding procedure they employ in producing the kittens they sell.

- Ask about their guarantees - A good breeder will be able to furnish you with guarantees about the health of a kitten and will not think twice about replacing sick kittens.

- Breeders who are not able to answer questions about the history of the cat should be eliminated from your list.

- Any person who claims to be a breeder but gives you dodgy answers and shady responses should be stricken off your list of people to deal with. A person who gives flowery promises is not ones you want to be dealing with as well. You need to be talking to someone who is upfront and honest.

- Pay close mind that you deal only with those who have been reputed to employ humane methods during their breeding process.

- Individuals who refuse to answer your questions, or who dodge them - there will be a select few who are only out to make money from you and are only concerned about your credit card going through. Eliminate them from your list.

- An upstanding breeder will have no qualms about allowing you to visit their facilities - Visiting breeders cattery will allow you to witness the cats in action in the environment they are in and you will most likely be able to determine how well the cats have been socialized.

- When given access to visit breeder's facilities you will be able to check out if the shelter kept clean.

- A breeder's transparency and willingness to attend to and answer your questions is a positive mark of an upstanding breeder and should be marked for strong consideration.

- Don't forget to ask about terms of payment and what guarantees the breeder has to offer. Once you are satisfied with your inquiries and you come to a decision ask about the breeder's terms, conditions and guarantees to seal the deal, payment and payment mode will be discussed. You will likely need to make a deposit for the kitten and will have to come back later when the time is right for the kitten/s to be separated from their mother.

Cat Shelters and Rescue - Adopt an Adult Himalayan Cat

Another option you may want to consider when looking for a Himalayan cat to take home is a cat shelter. Cat shelters may not always have the cat of your choice available but it is worth a try. Not only will you save a considerable amount of money at a cat shelter but you would also be doing a good deed of rescuing a Himalayan from an uncertain future.

A distinct and obvious difference of getting a Himalayan cat from a breeder and adopting one from a shelter is that you would have given the cat a good chance of being in a better home with the latter. The beauty of adopting an adult cat is that it would have been already socialized. The possibility of it being given the initial medical care is likely but not guaranteed. Because of the intelligence of a Himalayan cat, it will be easier to integrate the adult cat into your everyday life with ease. And even if they can't speak up and say so, the cat will be able to express its gratitude to you each day you share.

On Selecting a Healthy Himalayan Cat

You will be able to have a longtime companion with a Himalayan cat because it has been observed to live a span of about 15 years with proper care and nourishment. Keep in mind that they are susceptible to hereditary and genetic conditions, increasing the likelihood of illness later on; hence the importance of dealing with a reputable breeder is an imperative.

As long as you get a healthy breed of Himalayan you can be assured that the maintenance and upkeep of the cat will be minimal. Your initial investments go toward acquisition of the cat, periodical vet checkups, cat equipment and sundries as well as food. Make sure that you have a list of the things you will need to ensure the happy and comfortable home transition of your Himalayan cat before bringing it home.

Behavior around Humans: Himalayan cats are docile, amiable and generally friendly cats. Should the Himalayan you bring home be skittish or display aloofness, take it as a sign of abuse or mistreatment from its previous owners. Invest a little more time with your cat if this is the case. Keep in mind that your patience is vital during this time of introducing it to your household. Himalayan cats are intelligent beings and will soon understand that you have its best interest in mind.

Mobility: Check out the cat in its current living conditions. Make sure that you check that the cat is able to walk, is mobile and does not display any signs of pain when in motion. Swollen limbs are a sure sign of osteopathy. Should you opt to adopt a Himalayan with an existing injury or genetic medical condition you should be ready to commit to frequent medical bills and regular visits to the vet.

Tail: It has a shorter tail as compared to most other cats that have long, tapered ones. There should be no bend in its tail. A bent tail signals that the cat could be prone to osteoarthritis, a painful, degenerative bone condition.

Cat-friendly Pet Interaction: You will be required to be present when you first introduce the new cat to your household. Give your Himalayan cat the chance to roam, get to know and discover the new environment on its own and supervise forays outdoors. Upon the introduction of new pets to members of the family, take time out to be present for this milestone. An investment of your time will be crucial to the integration of your cat to the home. Keep in mind that the Himalayan cat is not the best choice to put into a mix of a noisy, boisterous household and if this is what your house is like you will need to pay mind to keep the peace.

Appetite: Himalayan cats are moderately hardy eater. Avoid making the mistake of over feeding your Himmy. Any overweight individual will have difficulty getting about and will have suffered strain on their limbs if their diet is not watched.

Body Appearance: Check and examine the limbs and extremities of the Himmy you wish to take home. Make sure that the cat is free from scarring, open wounds, sores, rough patches, and bald spots. The body of the Himalayan is cobby and medium in build. If you can feel the bones through its skin then there is a possibility that it is malnourished and underfed.

Coat: Check for ticks and fleas that may have infested the coat of the Himmy. Himalayan cats have long, supple fur and this would be the opposite of a cat who is infested with ticks and mites.

Skin: Healthy skin is free from fungus patches and bald spots. Check that the skin of the Himmy you are taking home is free from skin infections or run the risk of passing a fungal infection to other pets.

Eyes: Discharge from the eyes signals respiratory problems in a cat. Check that the eyes of the Himmy are clear, alert and is free from discharge.

Ears: Check that the ears of the Himmy are wax free, mite free and clean. Keep a look out for tiny nicks or wounds that could lead to infection. Ear infections can be avoided through regular cleaning. .

Mouth and Teeth: Check for any mouth deformities, drooling or abnormalities such as protruding teeth.

Belly or Stomach: Check for swelling as well as lumps around the belly area.

Anal Area: Check and make sure that the anal area is clean, that there is no matting in that region of the body and that there is no sign of bleeding or discharge from the anal area.

Important Note

Reputable breeders will only hand over Himalayan kittens when they reach 12 weeks of age. It is strongly recommended that separation from its mother is held off until the kitten has weaned. Wait until the kitten is ready to eat solid food before you take it home.

Chapter Five: Maintaining the Health of Your Himalayan Cat

Like other breeds of feline, Himalayan cats, depending on the breeding methods employed initial to their development, can be prone to some illnesses. Find out more about how you can keep your cat healthy in the next sections of this chapter. Committing to taking in a cat to raise is a big responsibility and undertaking. Part and parcel of this responsibility is to knowing any medical conditions which your Himalayan cat may be prone.

As your cat's trusted caregiver it will be up to you to recognize any signs of discomfort, distress, pain or unease your Himmy may display. They key to your Himmy's health and well-being hinges on the care and attention you and equally responsible caregivers extend to it. With proper maintenance from its owners the Himalayan cat could thrive well and live in a long and happy contended life of about 15 years. Their chances look better when they are embraced in an environment of loving care and good companionship. The next sections of this chapter hope to carefully show what an owner needs to look out for in terms of the Himalayan cat's health care and grooming maintenance.

Grooming Your Himalayan Cat

These colorfully long-haired cats with a usually flat face may look mean and angry because of their pinched look, but they are some of the most quiet and even-tempered cats around. Their long thick fur is rich and luxurious and should be brushed daily in order to avoid any knotting, tangling or matting of the fur.

Avoid periodontal disease and brush your cat's teeth at least once a week. However it would be better if this can be done at least every other day - better yet, daily. Comb through your cat's fur once a week to help remove dead fur. Doing so will help avoid matting and essentially, distribute skin oils for better skin promotion. Not only will you avoid medical bills due to poor skin conditions, you and your Himmy will also be making good memories during downtime.

They need to be brushed daily using a comb or a soft brush. Do this carefully and slowly as any tangling in the fur may cause them pain when doing so. Keep your Himmy cat indoors to avoid it from picking up dirt on its dense fur. Should you allow getting some sunshine and allowing it outdoors, making sure that these are short trips outside and that they are supervised to avoid them from possible big animal attacks. Remember to give it a gentle brushing at least once a day to remove debris it may have picked up during its time outside.

Trimming Nails

Since your Himalayan cat will mostly remain indoors, it is best to provide it a scratching post where it can help trim down its nails. Should you deem it fit to trim your Himmy's nails, it is best to get them used to filing. Filing down of its nails will reduce the sharpness of its claws.

You may also use a round-ended pair of clippers to clip the ends of its nails. To do this, take your Himmy's paw and lightly press on it to expose each nail. Clip its nails above the pink line called the quick. Avoid accidental bleeding by swaddling your Himmy in a warm blanket while doing this. Wrap them up like a burrito in order to make the procedure a safer one for cat.

Wrapping them in a blanket will not only allow you to cut their nails safely it will also provide them a bit of comfort during the procedure. The sooner your Himmy gets used to regular grooming routines the better it will allow you to carry out these grooming tasks. You will be able to discover a technique best for you and your Himalayan as you get to know each other.

Proper Oral Hygiene for Your Himalayan Cat

This will not be a favorite activity for your Himmy or for most other felines for that matter. But brushing your cat's teeth will need to be done in order to keep its pearly whites and mouth clean and odor free. Food debris stuck in between its teeth will likely promote dental problems for the cat.

Just like you it needs a good mouth cleaning. Use mild toothpaste and a soft toothbrush specifically made for cats. Unlike you, your cat will only need to have its teeth cleaned at least once a week. Make tooth brushing a part of the groom-time routine with your Himalayan cat.

Bathing Your Himalayan Cat

Acclimate your cat to bathing regularly. Because of its long, rich coat, it will be unavoidable for your Himmy to pick up dirt and debris on its fur. It is best to give your cat a warm bath at least two to three times a month to keep its long fur silky smooth. Be sure that you ask your vet about shampoo and soap best suited for their kind. Introduce water to your Himmy by dropping a few droplets onto its paw. Cup your hands and gently wet the feet, underside and bottom of your cat. Lather soap or cat shampoo in your hands and gently rub your Himalayan cat's fur until the soap is a mild lather. Keep in mind to use soap that is pet-approved when giving your Himalayan cats a bath. Rinse your cat off by gently lowering your Himmy in a basin or tub of warm water.

Make sure that you thoroughly dry them after the bath using warm soft towels. Under no circumstance should they be allowed to walk around damp. This will cause them to catch cold and is not good for their poor respiratory system.

Cleaning Your Himmy's Face and Ears

Use a damp cloth to wipe down the face of your Himalayan cat especially after meals. Because of their pinched faces, Himmies tend to pick up food debris that gets stuck between the folds of their faces. Do the same when cleaning their ears. Using a soft, damp cloth, lightly wipe the insides of your Himmy's ears to avoid wax build up and to check for mite infestation.

Chapter Six: Breeding Matters

Explicitly bred for the cat fancy, work on establishing the combined breed of the Persian and Siamese cats began in the United States at the Harvard University and the outcome was later published in 1936 in the Journal of Heredity. None of the major cat fancier groups at that time gave recognition to the cats until it was independently developed by Brian Sterling-Webb. Sterling-Webb cross bred the cats for a span of a decade in the United Kingdom, and was given recognition in 1955 as the Longhaired Colourpoint granted by the Governing Council of the Cat Fancy (GCCF).

A separate effort on breeding the cat was simultaneously happening across the pond in the United States by a fancier only known as Mrs. Goforth. The Himalayan was granted recognition by the Cat Fanciers Association in 1957.

The early breeders of the Longhaired Colourpoint was predominantly interested in giving the cat the colouration of the Siamese cat and the stock was only outbred to Persian cats to keep the dominance of the Persian's traits. It was in the 1960's the Siamese stock was reintroduced to the breeding development which produced less of the Persian-looking cats. The 1980's saw efforts to re-establish the breed to the formally Persian lines which called for the breed to be merged into registries, like the CFA, as a variant of the Persian cat.

There have been more than 343, 000 Himalayan cats registered in registries since 1957. 2, 428 Himalayans have been shown in 1998 with an average of 5.6 Himalayan kitten entries per show. It has received regional awards over 175 times since 1992 and has achieved over 21 national awards since 1981. Breeders of Himalayan cats, especially those registered with one or more cat fancier associations like the CFA, or The International Cat Association (TICA)are requires to follow a strict code of ethics as well as breeding guidelines to ensure a healthy lot.

These members are required to mind the care and the legitimacy of the Himalayan cat's bloodlines. Should you find a local area breeder, call to make an appointment and pay a visit to the cattery. Meeting the breeder and kittens in person is the best way to surmise the methods employed by the breeder and the cattery when they develop and produce their cats.

Should the breeder from a faraway place, you could check out their website and study the history of their winning show cats as well as customer reviews and testimonials. You want to be able to study the track record of a breeder and determine whether they do adhere to the precepts and ethics of the associations of which they are members.

All Himalayan cats, to some extent, are affected by a serious condition called Brachycephaly. Each time a brachycephalic kitten is sold, breeders of this sort is encouraged to continue develop more flat-faced kittens. This is a grave concern for many feline advocacy groups and registries who have called for and advocate changes to the breed standards of the Himalayan cat.

Once known as the Feline Advisory Bureau, the International Cat Care has stated that a multitude of medical problems arise from breeding cats that are flat-faced.

This in turn results in the harming of the cat by opting to breed them in this manner. This is certainly something important to consider prior to acquiring any flat faced breed of animal, specially the charmingly adorable Himalayan.

Should you be decided on the Himalayan cat, think about adopting or rescuing an adult that has been abandoned. You may also seek out less extreme line breed. Unlike Persian cats, Himalayan cats do not have to be flat faced in order to be shown therefore you can purchase a more round faced Himalayan. This reduces respiratory risks and complications.

Chapter Seven: Nutritional Needs of Your Himalayan Cats

Himalayan cats like other felines are meat-eaters and thrives on a meat-based diet. This is important to know and mind whilst pondering on your decision. If this is not adhered to then you and your cat may face a long road of frustration and/or harmful food experimentation. Be sure to choose a few meat varieties to feed your Himalayan cat so that it does not get bored eating the same thing over and over again. Just like you and i, your Himmy will appreciate variety in its diet so offer it different types of meat dishes.

Try out small portions of boiled chicken or beef, and alternate this with a nutritionally balanced commercial dry cat food. Consult with your vet about the amount of food you should give to your cat. Its weight and age will play a factor in the amount of food it will need to be fed.

The next section will give information on the portion, ratio and types of foods you can serve your Himalayan cat. We will discuss what you need to feed your cat to raise it successfully and medically-sound. We will also discuss foods that your Himalayan cat can and can't eat.

The Nutritional Needs of Himalayan Cats

Himalayan cats are meat-eaters. Its diet is limited and if not given the proper foods may seem like finicky eaters. The Himalayan cat is a carnivore much like its big cat cousins. Its diet has to be rich in protein, fats and meats. Himalayan cats, like most other cat breeds, will not take well to carbohydrates. Avoid giving it any foods that have artificial colouring and additives as this could spell disaster on its digestive system. Sharing ancestry with big, wild cats, Himalayan cats will thrive best on a diet rich with meat. It is not a vegetarian and it will not get the nutrition it needs with vegetables. Sure, you may try to give it a treat or two with carrot sticks but do not expect them to welcome shrubbery or vegetables.

Cats thrive best on smaller portions given in scheduled portions throughout the day. Be sure to consult your vet as to how much food is the right amount to furnish the cat. Once you know how much to feed your Himmy, you should stick to this regimen as religiously as possible. Your Himalayan cat may seem hungry all the time and you may think that you are underfeeding it, but sticking to the prescribed portions your vet recommends will work best for its health in the long run.

Continue feeding your growing kitten cereals, oats, wheat, and calcium rich dairy products whilst you slowly introduce meats to its meals. Continue mixing in a yolk of egg in your Himalayan cat's meals at least twice a week. Acceptable meats include boiled chicken, beef and liver. Do not serve your growing kitten pork or lamb. You may add variety by adding a bit of boiled brown rice, some whole grain wheat, cereals or buckwheat with the slivers of meat. Make sure that your meat portions are larger than the cereals.

Iron will be a recommended addition to your cat's diet. Liver will be a good source of much needed iron for your juvenile Himalayan. It is recommended that you provide your Himmy a small portion of liver with its meals at least once a month. Boil some liver in water then chop it up or run it through a food processor.

You can mix the liver in with the usual boiled chicken or beef. Add a smaller portion of oats to the mix to give your cat a balanced diet. You will notice that your Himalayan cat's feeding frequency will radically lessen in terms of frequency. When you once had to feed your cat 5-6 times a day, you will notice that this will be cut in half as your Himalayan cat matures.

Protein

Be sure that introduce meats or meat-based products to lessen the impact of stress on guardian and cat. Do not think that your Himalayan cat is eats like you, because they are not going to fare well if given the additives, preservatives, seasonings and food colouring that are usually present in human food.

Taurine

Do introduce taurine to your Himalayan cat's food. Taurine is an essential amino acid that is required by all felines.

Cereals

You can mash up a small portion of buckwheat, oat, whole grain or brown cereal to its meat diet. But be sure that this is minimal in portion.

Carbohydrates

Cats do not respond well to carbohydrates and so with your Himalayan. It may not refuse it giving you a false sense of security that if it eats it, the food must be acceptable. This is not so. Carbohydrates in the diet of a feline tend to make them obese and they may possibly develop diabetes if given carbohydrates. Keep in mind that you need to avoid giving your Himalayan cat carbohydrates in its diet.

Water

Water is an essential part of your Himalayan cat's diet and daily needs. Be sure that you always set out a fresh bowl of clean water for your cat. Replenish its water bowl at least twice a day and keep a close look out that it drinks regularly. Cats are not eager water drinkers but they will need to have water in order to lower their body temperature most especially during the warmer seasons of the year.

What Foods to Choose for Your Himalayan Cats

Himalayan cats are carnivores that will need protein and lots of it. This is a given, taking into account that they share ancestry with the much bigger cats of the wild. Within this section you will discover more about what sort of other foods you can and shouldn't give to your furry-faced feline buddy.

Avoid the long and painstaking process of finding out what your Himalayan cat prefers to eat by giving it small amounts of different varieties of food. Switch up the food you serve to it so that it does not get tired of eating just one sort of food. Giving it just one choice may likely make it bored of the diet it is served. This may be the cause of your cat refusing to eat which in turn could make it malnourished. If you opt to have backup commercial foods for busy days choose foods deemed acceptable by the American of Feed Control Officials.

A wiser choice as caregiver and guardian is to include cooking their meals when you cook yours. It isn't a tedious a process as you think it is and it ensures that you are feeding it food you have control over in terms of freshness, selection and preparation. You may also want to consider giving it home cooked foods if you have the luxury of time. Home cooked meals will ensure that you are giving it the proper portions of fresh meals. You will have better control of selection, preparation and you can be certain that what you feed your Himalayan cat is fresh and nutritionally sound. You will also discover, in the long run, that doing this will put less of a dent on your finances.

Feeding Your Grown Himalayan Cat

A lot of cat owners have made the mistake of figuring that their Himalayan cat's diet is not unlike ours. However, there is a big difference. It serves you well to know that your Himalayan cat thrives best nutritionally when fed a balanced diet. So as much as it will not eagerly gobble up a dish of vegetables it is wise to keep in mind that mixing in a bit of acceptable veggies like boiled cauliflower, green beans, mashed carrots to their usual fare of boiled and chopped up meats like chicken or beef is required for it to enjoy a healthy life.

The convenience of preparing home cooked meals for your cat in the comfort of your own kitchen is that you can do this when you cook for yourself or the family. You can even go on a weekend spree of cooking and prepare these dishes which you can cool, store and reheat for later consumption during the following week. You can be assured of the cleanliness, freshness and have control over the quality of food that you feed your cat. You will also be doing your finances a real solid by making this part of your routine at home.

Opting for Canned Food

There will be days when you will be too busy to prepare meals and will have to break into your stock of commercial cat food. It is perfectly acceptable to switch up your cat's meals with commercial brands as long as you make sure that the commercial food you get is nutritionally sound and balanced. Make sure that you choose cat food that has been approved by food security authorities. Canned and dry cat food inspected and approved by food security agency boards are wise choices. Choose to alternate canned or dry foods with home-cooked meals only when absolutely necessary.

When you rescue or adopt a Himalayan cat, it would serve you well to know what sort of food its former guardians had fed the cat. Especially the brand of dry or canned foods which the Himmy has been given before it joined you. You may have to continue feeding your new addition this way as you begin to switch up its diet to food that you prepare at home along with equally healthy and well balanced food choices that are store-bought.

Chapter Eight: Safety Tips on How to Feline – Proof Your Home

Himalayan cats are docile and amiable creatures with a pleasant and mild temperament, that being said, you will have to take it upon yourself to make sure that you cat-proof your home in order to create a safe space for you, your family and your new feline addition. You will need to keep your new ward safe as its new owner and family. Read on to find out how you can start preparing your home to welcome your new found friend.

Secure Your Family, Fort and Feline

- Keep all food items out of your cats reach and store them in cupboards or stack them up in a closed pantry. Make sure that any food taken out of the fridge or pantry is securely covered or sealed in a spill-proof container.

- Almost all felines have an innate curiosity in them and will investigate almost anything that is out in the open, most especially if they smell food somewhere. Keep them from tipping, spilling or pushing over garbage bins and make sure that all trash receptacles are tightly lidded and won't spill out in the event that your cat topples it over.

- Cats are curious and will usually play with small objects which they can roll around and play with if they come across any object that would capture their fancy. As a rule of thumb, keep all medication away from the reach of children and pets. Look up first aid tips that you can employ should your pet have an emergency.

- Make sure that medicine, vitamins, supplements and the likes are kept out of your cat's reach. Accidental medicine ingestion by your cat is not a situation you want to deal with. Many, if not most human medicines can be dangerously toxic if not fatal to cats. Aspirin and paracetamol are some of the more dangerous pills that you should keep out of your cats reach.

- Keep little baubles and valuables stored away because your little fur ball is the kind of feline who likes to play with shiny things. You certainly would not want your Himmy to swallow something tiny and have it lodge in their throat. Should this happen bring your feline to the vet immediately.

- Wrap wires in protective plastic wore covers to avoid your cat from gnawing at it. Not doing so may lead to electrocution.

- Make certain that ropes from curtains or blinds are out of your Himmy reach. Even a mild-manned Himalayan could get into occasional mischief and get entangled in these ropes.

- Cats have a natural tendency to scrounge, rummage and hunt for its food. Avoid messy kitchen spills by making sure all trash cans are covered tightly.

- Cleaning products contain a host of toxic chemicals which are poisonous and can cause dire harm your new pet. Avoid running the risk of your cat getting to these products as ingestion or inhalation can cause them to get ill or worse. Keep all cleaning products stored away where your kitten can't get to them.

- Most plants are toxic to felines. Take stock of the plants around the perimeter of your home and should there be any poisonous plants like calla lily or deadly nightshade that flank your home, you want to replace them with safer plants. Poisoning from toxic plants or harmful ingestion by cats is a very real medical concern.

- It is not unusual for cats to get carried away when they are at play and they can be quite a handful especially when you have more than one pet. Avoid electrocution by using plastic socket covers to close electric plug sockets.

- Cats and string go hand in hand and they do have a knack for gnawing at anything that mimics string. Wires are best kept away from them or covered up. Earphones and charger cables should be stored away from where they can be reached by your curious cat. Save yourself the hassle and the money of replacing chargers cables and earphones in the long run.

Chapter Eight: Safety Tips on How to Feline – Proof Your Home

Chapter Nine: Living With Your New Himalayan Cat

     The Himalayan cat is one of the most popular choices of cats for many feline aficionados and they have been appreciated and enjoyed by many since they were first developed in the 1930's. The idea of taking in a pet may look and sound easier than it is but in fact a lot of patience and love during the transition of introducing your new furry friend into the family is a big requirement at the beginning of the relationship. Understand that in any home dynamics, taking in a new pet means a period of adjustment for all concerned.

This is why you are called the caregiver because the success of a peaceful integration will be resting on your shoulders. Empower yourself with the basic information on providing a safe, happy and healthy home to your new Himalayan Cat. This section aims to guide you on how to furnish and set up safe spaces and areas around your house for your cat and its basic, everyday needs.

Activity and Habitat for Himalayan Cats

Each cat is different from one another in personality and character and just like us each of them thrive in homes where they feel safe, loved, protected and cared for by their humans. The Himalayan cat may be mild-mannered, charming, amiable and easy-to-get-along-with feline but this doesn't mean that it couldn't get into mischief sometimes. It is important to remember that physical stimulation with proper toys and props should be employed on a regular basis.

It is recommended to keep Himalayan cats indoors and raise them inside the safety and comfort of your home. Their cobby physique along with their unique colour point markings makes them fancy eye-catchers and they will turn heads. Allowing them unsupervised trips outdoors could have them fall into the wrong hands. Yes, there are real cat-nappers out there.

This is also a good time to take stock of the greenery and foliage that surround your home. Pay mind that you are aware of any toxic plants that the cat may munch on which in turn could cause it to become ill and serious medical repercussions.

Keeping Your Himalayan Cat Healthy and Fit

Make time for playtime and engage your Himalayan in gentle play. Because Himalayan Cats are less inclined to exercise on their own, it will be up to you and other people in your home or family to have frequent interaction with the new family addition. Obesity is a real problem your Himalayan cat may suffer from if they are not given the proper stimulation and exercise that occur during playtime. Cats are typically playful pets that enjoy chasing lasers, feather teasers, run after soft, bouncy balls and plush toys. These are some of the recommended toys for the cat to play with rather than playing with them using your bare hands.

A scratching post or two shall have to be provided for the cat and you will need to find a place around your home where you can strategically place these posts - unless you are ready to live with the clawed-looked on your favourite furniture. Do refer back to the chapter which discusses cat-proofing your home.

Equipment You Need to Supply Your Himalayan Cat

Litter Boxes

Properly welcoming and integrating your new Himmy at home will mean that you will have to provide spaces for it where it can go and do natures business and go potty. If your new cat is not housebroken, fret not because Himalayan cats are clever and one of the breeds that are easier to train to go to the toilet where it's supposed.

Make sure that you strategically place litter boxes in non-chaotic, semi-busy areas around the house where they are tucked away but accessible to the cat, a hidden but busy hallway, one under an indoor, toxic-free, preferably decorative plant. Another in a corner of the family room and an extra one to boot in the toilet area would be ideal places to place litter boxes where the cat can be comfortable to do natures business.

Cat Litter

Pet supply shops carry a plethora of varied choices of scented cat litter that will keep hygiene and odor in check. Be sure to shovel out cat poop from litter boxes at least twice a day. Cats hate going in a litter box full of doo doo. As a rule of thumb, the ratio of cats to litter boxes is 1:2. This ensures that cats will have no qualms about doing their business when nature calls. Remember to throw out soiled cat litter and replace this regularly.

Cat Carrier

You will need to transport your Himalayan cat periodically; when you go for medical checkups or when going to the groomer for routine coat maintenance. A cat carrier will help safely transport your cat from point A to point B and will minimize the cat stress.

Cat Brush

Invest on a good brush which will come in handy for down time bonding and to massage your cat. Moderately frequent brushing will also help get the cat's skin oils circulating better allowing its fur to remain silky-soft. This will be an especially important part of your daily routine once you take home your long-haired Himalayan cat because you will need to keep its fur tangle-free through frequent brushing.

Cat Toys

Plush balls are great cat toy ideas. Plush toys are easy for your gentle cat to munch on and will be easy for you to throw around. Soft toys are easy to chase after. Other safe cat toys are feather-teasers, bells, reward-giving toys as well as a sturdy scratching post or two are in order to help keep its physical exercise in check.

Cat Bed

Pick out a nice, soft, warm and comfy bed for your Himmy to sleep, curl into, warm up in and laze about. Set out a soft mat on your screened in yard deck, patio or porch where your Himmy can soak in some rays and enjoy a nice breeze as you enjoy the day with it.

Food and Water Dishes

Get rid of plastic feeding dishes and opt for ceramic or stainless bowls for their food and water.

Scratching Post

All felines will tend to sharpen their claws by scratching and clawing at random objects around your house. To avoid furniture destruction procures a couple of scratching posts which you should place strategically in areas around your home.

Toothbrush

Ask a an experienced owner or a veterinarian to teach and show you how to properly brush your Himmy's teeth and be sure to snag a cat toothbrush for your new house mate along with the other stuff you're already going to get.

Kitten and Cat Supplies

Breeders, usually the ones of good repute, will hand over little extras to you for your kitten, like feeding bowls, toys and other stuff used by your Himmy while under their care. These are other things you will have to purchase or put aside money for as you get ready to welcome your Himalayan cat home:

- Vaccination for kittens: $50 - $100
- Vet visit: $35 - $50
- Kitten Food: $15-$30

- Treats: $5 - $15
- Drinking and feeding bowls: $50 - $150
- Brush and comb (get one of each): $7 - $50
- Bed and blankets: $25 - $100
- Clippers and Trimmers: $6 - $50
- Liners and mats: $2 - $40
- Litter Boxes: $15 - $200
- Kitty Litter: $5 - $35
- Scratching posts $50-$200
- Filters and deodorants: $4 - $25
- Waste Disposal: $3 - $30
- Toy Crate: $10 - $150
- Cat carrier: $25 - $200
- Toys: $1 - $50
- Tooth brush $5-$10
- Vet approved toothpaste $10-$15
- Vet approved pet cologne $20-$30

Good to Know When Acquiring Cat Supplies

Expect these prices to vary depending on your preference and budget. Prices will differ variably depending on where you purchase. It is best to get these all sorted out early on so that you can start organizing spaces in your home and move things around if needed.

Make sound investments on the equipment and sundries your Himalayan cat will need because it will be using these items regularly and you want them to last. Pay mind that you clean these items on a regular basis to get rid of fur balls, remove dust accumulation, and other undesirable matter.

We recommend shallow, stainless steel or porcelain bowls for feeding and eating since cat whiskers get in the way. Slow feeding bowls allow your cat to eat at a pace and not have it scarf down their food too fast. You could also get one of those fancy cat feeders which train your cat to release only a certain amount of food at a time - this helps to prevent overeating as well.

Speaking of food, the quality of food will greatly play a big factor on your cat's health and wellness. Be sure that you choose just a bit of food at the beginning. You want to serve it bits of food at a time so that you can figure out which they prefer. Make sure that the food you choose will give them the optimum balance in nutrition. Not only will balanced nutrition serve them well physically, it will also optimize them mentally.

Monthly Costs

The monthly expenses of raising your Himalayan cat should be relatively more consistent as the months and years go by. So long as they are healthy you will not need to spend as much money as you initially did because you would have already invested in the necessary sturdy sundries.

Don't get caught spending outside of your income because this will be a source of frustration. You need to get your finances sorted out and figure out the monthly costs of raising your Himalayan cats before they arrive. Here is a short list of what you could expect to spend each month after acquisition.

- Kitten Food: $15-$30
- Treats: $5 - $15
- Kitty Litter: $5 - $35
- Waste Disposal: $3 - $30
- Liners and mats: $2 - $40
- Filters and deodorants: $4 - $25

Don't scrimp on supplies your new pet will need. Invest in sturdy products and pay no mind to all the marketing hype. Choosing the proper, sturdy sundries could save a hefty sum in the long run.

Ask around and get tips from other cat guardians on where to get reliable equipment for your Himalayan cat buddy. There will be many products that will boast of being "top sellers" but won't make the cut in terms of quality or durability. Again, don't get carried away by the hype. Check out pet websites which sell pet products and read through the ratings and comments of their customers to get a better idea of the products they manufacture.

Pay attention and learn to understand the labels of products you consider before buying them for your pet. As much as there are many good pet merchandize out there, there is equally a number of pet product manufacturers who are merely out to make a profit. Many pet equipment producers use low grade materials that do not pass quality standards. There are others which use chemicals that pose a toxic threat to your Himalayan cat and your family. Do not make the mistake of buying second hand equipment for your Himmy. You need to keep in mind that cats get anxious when they sniff out a strange scent. It is best to invest in affordably new, sturdy equipment for your cat's needs.

The responsibility of owning a pet entails a lot of details that will require your attention and action. Your extensive research will give you some peace of mind.

Chapter Ten: Common Diseases, Temperament and Color Points

Due to the Himalayan cat being from the same gene pool as Persians, the cat has been noted to have tendency to suffer from a few breed-based health issues and is similarly prone to medical conditions as the Persian cat. These include breathing and sinus problems which are due to its short, snub-nosed face as well as the development of shorter sinus cavities. This chapter will cover some of the most common diseases of Himalayan cats as well as their different types and color points. You'll also get to learn more about their temperament.

Common Diseases

Its Persian roots cause the Himmie to be susceptible to Polycystic Kidney Disease (PKD) which is a congenital disease. This is a disease where cysts develop in the kidneys of the long-haired cat and slowly enlarges as the cat matures. Early detection can prevent the disease from developing further and can be managed through specially thought out diets which assist in reducing the cat's kidneys to get overworked. In the event of the disease progressing overtime, this may lead to terminal kidney disease later on so it is absolutely important that the Himalayan cat get tested early on to avoid and avert this from developing further.

Eye, liver and skin problems are also noted to be more common with Himalayan cats than in other breed mixes. So if you are bent on getting a Himmie to take home with you, you shall need to prepare to screen your cat twice annually to determine any issues that may later come along.

Himalayans share more of the Persian gene generally, giving them the distinct appearance of cobby bodies and short legs. Their shorter stems make it harder for the

Himmies to jump about like other cats. It was only in the 1960's when some Himmie was observed to have a more Siamese - looking physique, ridding the feline of leaping limitations. However, these longer-stemmed cats may be prevented from being shown in some associations due to the specific breed standards of the organization.

The Colour Points, Types and Appearances of A Himalayan Cat

In Britain the Himalayan cat is called a Colourpoint Persian or a Coloutrpoint Longhair. It is said to be the second most popular cat worldwide and can reach up to 12 pounds in weight. It is a cat with luxuriously long, dense coat that is white to faw in colour. Its face, as well as ears, feet and tails - called points - are typically darker in colours of lilac, chocolate, red or blue.

They are the result of cross breeding of the Siamese with the Persian cat. Himmies are considered a Colourpoint Longhair or a type of Persian cat by the Cat Fancier's Association, meaning that they have a lot of the endearing traits of the Persian cat. All Himmies come in varied colours of lilac, chocolate, blue, flame, cream and seal. They can also come in colours of red-point and tortoise-point.

It has a round head that is large and cobby. It has a flat face
and rounded ear points. Its head sits atop a stubby neck set
above a muscular physique carried by short, stubby legs
with a short tail.

Himalayan cats sport round, cobby physiques with
short legs, making it more difficult for them to leap like most
other cats. This appearance of the Himalayan has changed
quite a bit since the 1960's when Siamese cats were used in
cross breeding procedures. However, there are a few
registries which do not find this body type acceptable for
show. Breed standards of specific organizations will have to
be inquired of to find out which body type they accept for
show cats.

Much like the Persian cat, the Himalayan has two
types - the more traditional doll-faced Himalayan and the
ultra-typed one with the more extreme, tight-looking facial
features. Himalayan show cats have a nose break like the
peke-faced Persian can and sport big, large, round eyes with
a leather nose break separating their eyes. Himalayan pet
cats typically have lengthier noses than those of the
traditional show cats.

A blue point Himalayan has a blue coat colour which
is confined to the points of its feet, tail, ears and face mask. A

lilac point Himalayan is a starker, more diluted version of the blue point with a fairer body colouration. A seal point is more a brown coloured cat whilst a chocolate point has concentrated colours around its face, tail, legs and ears. A distinction of body colour between the seal point and the chocolate point Himalayan can be found in the paws of the cats. Whilst the chocolate point will have pink pads for its paws, the seal point has brown paw pads.

The fur of the Himalayan cat is either cream or white with points that come in varied colours of lilac, blue, red, chocolate, seal and cream. There are also occurrences of points being tabby, tortoiseshell and lynx in pattern. Chocolate and lilac Himalayans are more challenging to create since both tom and queen has to have the chocolate/lilac gene in order to produce the same coloured kitten.

Temperament and Personality

Himalayans are intelligent, sociable, sweet-tempered and make excellent companions. They are more active than their Persian ancestors and fare better as indoor cats. They are a playful sort who is gentle and calm in demeanor. They love to play with their humans and can even be trained to play fetch. They are not at all high maintenance in terms of wanting attention and will be happy to amuse themselves for hours on end with simple toys that would engage them.

Unlike other cats who like to perch atop high places, Himalayan cats have little inclination to scramble up kitchen counters, cabinet tops or high shelves. They are not likely to clamber up curtains or leap from high places because of their shorter limbs.

It has a musical lilt to its voice and expresses itself softly. It has a pleasant disposition and a non-aggressive nature. Keeping them indoors would be the best for them since they are not able to defend themselves. Whilst they have a laid back manner about them, they aren't what you would call lazy since they do enjoy playtime very much. They are not made to be working animals and are best kept as lap and indoor pets.

Much like their Siamese kin, they can get pretty chatty and will attempt to make light conversation with you. They are well balanced cats who like to divide their time between playtime and lounging. They are a loving sort who does not possess a mean bone and make good pets for couples, families or singles.

Care Sheet and Summary

This chapter will cover a quick overview of the lessons you've learned and the points you need to remember when keeping Himalayan cats. We hope that you enjoy many days of warm cuddling and endless joy as you bring home your very own amiably docile, cuddly, wide-eyed, affectionate and amusingly cobby Himalayan cat.

A Summary of Facts about the Himalayan Cat

- **Pedigreed:** by the Cat Fanciers' Association, TICA, and AACE
- **Breed Size:** Medium
- **Height:** 10 - 15 inches (25 - 38 cm) tall
- **Weight:** 7 - 15 lbs. for both male and females
- **Coat Texture:** medium to long fur
- **Color:** blue-point, lilac-point, seal-point, chocolate point
- **Eyes:** expressively round close-set eyes that could be in hues of green, blue and gold.

- **Temperament:** Intelligent, sweet-tempered and amiable. The Himalayan needs moderate attention and adores being around its humans and interacting with them. Although notably more active than their Persian ancestors, Himalayan cats are still best suited for calm, relaxed families and individuals. Bonds with a few select members of a family and enjoys attentive, cuddle, lap time with their chosen humans.

- **Strangers and New Environments:** guarded but fairly sociable once it considers the person to be trust-worthy; does not do well with frequent changes in its environment.

- **Other Pets:** with the owners patient integration it could adapt well with other existing cat friendly pets you may own

- **Training:** Highly trainable and adapts easily to people who handle them gently.

- **Playtime Needs:** frequent, active playtime exercise is encouraged strongly for Himalayan cats.

- **Health Conditions:** Himalayan cats, because of their Persian ancestry are prone to polycystic kidney disease but can be managed through neutering or spaying as well as diet.

- **Grooming needs:** Himalayan cat needs daily fur brushing to promote healthy skin and coat. Their faces also need to be wiped daily to avoid skin infections. Regular bathing is recommended to aid the reduction of skin oils on the skin and fur.

- **Lifespan:** typical average lifespan is 8-15 years

Basic Nutritional Information of the Himalayan Cat

- **Nutritional Needs** - diet rich in meats (chicken or beef), grains, oats, egg yolks, protein, calcium from cream cheese, yogurt, buttermilk, iron from liver.

- **Water Consumption** - frequent replenishment of water dish is advised.

- **Feeding Amount** - varies on specific factors like history, gender, weight, size, age.

- **Feeding Frequency** - It is best to consult with your vet about the amount of food you put out for your cat.

- **Mixed Foods** - include allowed veggies like carrots, broccoli into meals.

- **Grains** - be sure to include grains and oats in its diet.

Breeding Information

- **Heat period**- two to three weeks
- **Female Sexual Maturity** - 4-12 months
- **Male Sexual Maturity** - 5 months

- **Female Breeding Age** - 14 months
- **Male Breeding Age** - 16 months
- **Litter Size** - about 3 - 4 kittens
- **Birth Interval** - 15 – 30 minutes
- **Pregnancy** – 64 - 67 days

Cat Accessories

- Litter boxes
- Cat litter
- Poop scooper or small plastic pail and shovel
- Scratching posts
- Cat bed
- Blanket
- Travel bag or Cat carrier
- Cat toys
- Feeding bowls
- Brush
- Toothbrush

Glossary of Cat Terms

Abundism – Referring to a cat that has markings more prolific than is normal.

Acariasis – A type of mite infection.

ACF – Australian Cat Federation

Affix – A cattery name that follows the cat's registered name; cattery owner, not the breeder of the cat.

Agouti – A type of natural coloring pattern in which individual hairs have bands of light and dark coloring.

Ailurophile – A person who loves cats.

Albino – A type of genetic mutation which results in little to no pigmentation, in the eyes, skin, and coat.

Allbreed – Referring to a show that accepts all breeds or a judge who is qualified to judge all breeds.

Alley Cat – A non-pedigreed cat.

Alter – A desexed cat; a male cat that has been neutered or a female that has been spayed.

Amino Acid – The building blocks of protein; there are 22 types for cats, 11 of which can be synthesized and 11 which must come from the diet (see essential amino acid).

Anestrus – The period between estrus cycles in a female cat.

Any Other Variety (AOV) – A registered cat that doesn't conform to the breed standard.

ASH – American Shorthair, a breed of cat.

Back Cross – A type of breeding in which the offspring is mated back to the parent.

Balance – Referring to the cat's structure; proportional in accordance with the breed standard.

Barring – Describing the tabby's striped markings.

Base Color – The color of the coat.

Bicolor – A cat with patched color and white.

Blaze – A white coloring on the face, usually in the shape of an inverted V.

Bloodline – The pedigree of the cat.

Brindle – A type of coloring, a brownish or tawny coat with streaks of another color.

Castration – The surgical removal of a male cat's testicles.

Cat Show – An event where cats are shown and judged.

Cattery – A registered cat breeder; also, a place where cats may be boarded.

CFA – The Cat Fanciers Association.

Cobby – A compact body type.

Colony – A group of cats living wild outside.

Color Point – A type of coat pattern that is controlled by color point alleles; pigmentation on the tail, legs, face, and ears with an ivory or white coat.

Colostrum – The first milk produced by a lactating female; contains vital nutrients and antibodies.

Conformation – The degree to which a pedigreed cat adheres to the breed standard.

Cross Breed – The offspring produced by mating two distinct breeds.

Dam – The female parent.

Declawing – The surgical removal of the cat's claw and first toe joint.

Developed Breed – A breed that was developed through selective breeding and crossing with established breeds.

Down Hairs – The short, fine hairs closest to the body which keep the cat warm.

DSH – Domestic Shorthair.

Estrus – The reproductive cycle in female cats during which she becomes fertile and receptive to mating.

Fading Kitten Syndrome – Kittens that die within the first two weeks after birth; the cause is generally unknown.

Feral – A wild, untamed cat of domestic descent.

Gestation – Pregnancy; the period during which the fetuses develop in the female's uterus.

Guard Hairs – Coarse, outer hairs on the coat.

Harlequin – A type of coloring in which there are van markings of any color with the addition of small patches of the same color on the legs and body.

Inbreeding – The breeding of related cats within a closed group or breed.

Kibble – Another name for dry cat food.

Lilac – A type of coat color that is pale pinkish-gray.

Line – The pedigree of ancestors; family tree.

Litter – The name given to a group of kittens born at the same time from a single female.

Mask – A type of coloring seen on the face in some breeds.

Matts – Knots or tangles in the cat's fur.

Mittens – White markings on the feet of a cat.

Moggie – Another name for a mixed breed cat.

Mutation – A change in the DNA of a cell.

Muzzle – The nose and jaws of an animal.

Natural Breed – A breed that developed without selective breeding or the assistance of humans.

Neutering – Desexing a male cat.

Open Show – A show in which spectators are allowed to view the judging.

Pads – The thick skin on the bottom of the feet.

Particolor – A type of coloration in which there are markings of two or more distinct colors.

Patched – A type of coloration in which there is any solid color, tabby, or tortoiseshell color plus white.

Pedigree – A purebred cat; the cat's papers showing its family history.

Pet Quality – A cat that is not deemed of high enough standard to be shown or bred.

Piebald – A cat with white patches of fur.

Points – Also color points; markings of contrasting color on the face, ears, legs, and tail.

Pricked – Referring to ears that sit upright.

Purebred – A pedigreed cat.

Queen – An intact female cat.

Roman Nose – A type of nose shape with a bump or arch.

Scruff – The loose skin on the back of a cat's neck.

Selective Breeding – A method of modifying or improving a breed by choosing cats with desirable traits.

Senior – A cat that is more than 5 but less than 7 years old.

Sire – The male parent of a cat.

Solid – Also self; a cat with a single coat color.

Spay – Desexing a female cat.

Stud – An intact male cat.

Tabby – A type of coat pattern consisting of a contrasting color over a ground color.

Tom Cat – An intact male cat.

Tortoiseshell – A type of coat pattern consisting of a mosaic of red or cream and another base color.

Tri-Color – A type of coat pattern consisting of three distinct colors in the coat.

Tuxedo – A black and white cat.

Unaltered – A cat that has not been desexed.

Index

L

M

N

Photo Credits

References

Are Himalayan Cats Mean Tempered? – The Nest.com
http://pets.thenest.com/himalayan-cats-mean-tempered-3672.html

Cat Breeds: Getting Cats to Get Along – PetCareRx.com
https://www.petcarerx.com/article/cat-breeds-getting-cats-to-get-along/825

Himalayan – CatTime.com
http://cattime.com/cat-breeds/himalayan-cats#/slide/1

Himalayan – CatTime.com
http://cattime.com/cat-breeds/himalayan-cats

Himalayan Cats - PetInsurance.com
https://phz8.petinsurance.com/pet-breeds/cat-breeds/himalayan

Himalayan Cats - Wikipedia.org
https://en.wikipedia.org/wiki/Himalayan_cat

Himalayan Cat – A Guide to the Breed - TheHappyCatSite.com
https://www.thehappycatsite.com/himalayan-cat/

Himalayan Cat Facts - SoftSchools.com
http://www.softschools.com/facts/cats/himalayan_cat_facts/2
631/

How to Care for Himalayan Cats - Wikihow.com
https://www.wikihow.com/Care-for-Himalayan-Cats

The Himalayan Persian - CFA.org
http://www.cfa.org/Breeds/BreedsKthruR/Persian/PERHIM
Article(1999).aspx

What Is the Personality of a Himalayan Cat? - TheNest.com
https://pets.thenest.com/personality-himalayan-cat-
6627.html

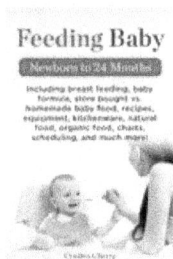

Feeding Baby
Cynthia Cherry
978-1941070000

Axolotl
Lolly Brown
978-0989658430

Dysautonomia, POTS
Syndrome
Frederick Earlstein
978-0989658485

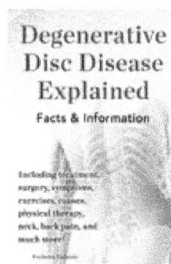

Degenerative Disc
Disease Explained
Frederick Earlstein
978-0989658485

Sinusitis, Hay Fever,
Allergic Rhinitis Explained
Frederick Earlstein
978-1941070024

Wicca
Riley Star
978-1941070130

Zombie Apocalypse
Rex Cutty
978-1941070154

Capybara
Lolly Brown
978-1941070062

Eels As Pets
Lolly Brown
978-1941070167

Scabies and Lice Explained
Frederick Earlstein
978-1941070017

Saltwater Fish As Pets
Lolly Brown
978-0989658461

Torticollis Explained
Frederick Earlstein
978-1941070055

Kennel Cough
Lolly Brown
978-0989658409

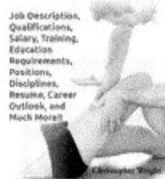

Physiotherapist, Physical
Therapist
Christopher Wright
978-0989658492

Rats, Mice, and Dormice
As Pets
Lolly Brown
978-1941070079

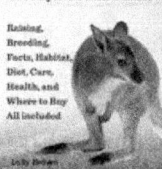

Wallaby and Wallaroo Care
Lolly Brown
978-1941070031

Bodybuilding Supplements
Explained
Jon Shelton
978-1941070239

Demonology
Riley Star
978-19401070314

Pigeon Racing
Lolly Brown
978-1941070307

Dwarf Hamster
Lolly Brown
978-1941070390

Cryptozoology
Rex Cutty
978-1941070406

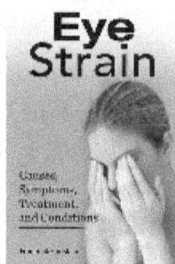

Eye Strain
Frederick Earlstein
978-1941070369

Inez The Miniature Elephant
Asher Ray
978-1941070353

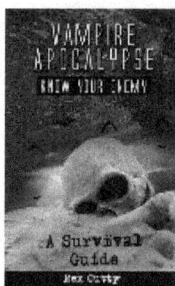

Vampire Apocalypse
Rex Cutty
978-1941070321